I CAN MAKE IT!

models

Ivan Bulloch

Series by Diane James & Sara Lynn

- **2** **Pebbles and Shells**
- **4** **Dancing Man**
- **6** **Monster Fun!**
- **8** **Animal Magic**
- **12** **Toy Town**
- **14** **Spotty Leopard**
- **16** **Salt Dough**
- **20** **Nodding Bird**
- **22** **Sticks and Stones**
- **24** **Index**

TWO-CAN

Pebbles and Shells

If you look around you – inside and outside – you will find lots of things to make models with. You can take your finds home and make models later, or you can make models on the spot! We made a collection of shells, pebbles and driftwood for the models on these pages.

Ready, steady, go...
1 Sort out your collection into things that would make good faces, eyes, noses or mouths.
2 Put the face shape down first. Then, lay the other features on top.

Dancing Man

If you follow the instructions here, you will be able to turn flat pieces of cardboard into moving models. You will need to buy a packet of 'split pins' from a stationery shop.

legs

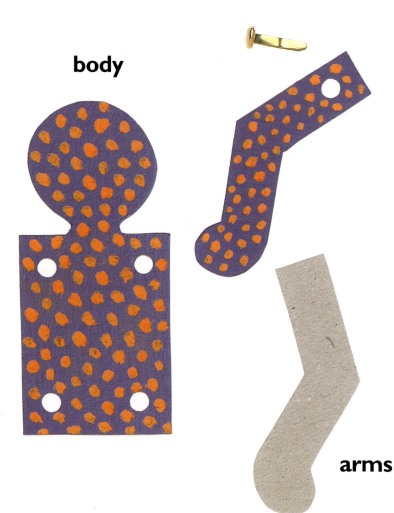
body

arms

5 Push a split pin through each hole in the body. Attach the legs and arms by pushing the pins through the holes in each piece.
6 Flatten the pins out to keep them in place.

Dancing Man
1 Trace around the body, leg and arm shapes on this page.
2 Cut the shapes out of cardboard.
3 Ask a grown-up to punch holes in all four corners of the body shape, and in the tops of the legs and arms.
4 Paint the shapes in bright colours.

Barking Dog
1 Trace around the dog shapes.
2 Punch two holes as shown.
3 Cut the shapes out, as before, from cardboard and paint them.
4 Use a split pin to hold the two shapes together.

mouth

dog

Monster Fun!

See how many different monsters you can make with just a few colours of play dough.

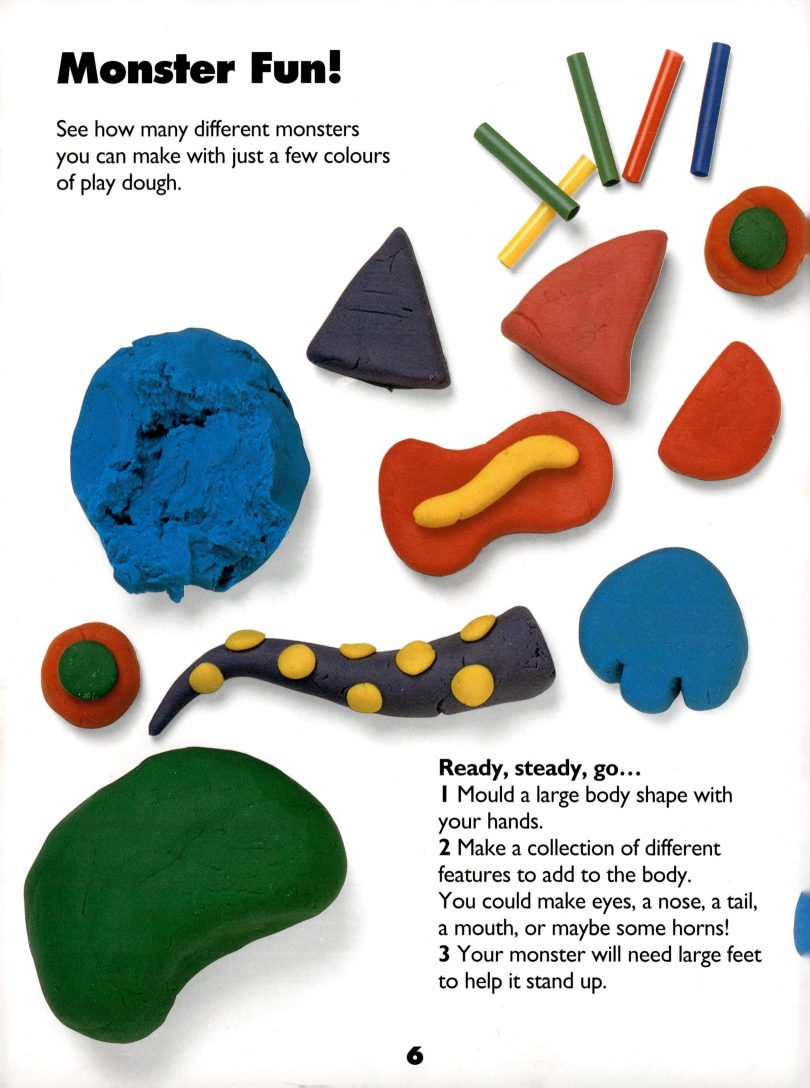

Ready, steady, go…
1 Mould a large body shape with your hands.
2 Make a collection of different features to add to the body. You could make eyes, a nose, a tail, a mouth, or maybe some horns!
3 Your monster will need large feet to help it stand up.

4 Cut some plastic straws into short lengths. Use the straws to attach the bits and pieces to your monster. Poke one end of the straw into the body and push another piece on to the other end.

5 When you have made a few monsters, you can take them apart and put them back together again in a different way!

Animal Magic

Here is a way to transform flat pieces of cardboard into an elephant that will stand up by itself!

Ready, steady, go…
1 Trace around the shapes on these pages.

2 Tape your traces to pieces of thick cardboard and cut out the shapes.

body

head

3 To make a complete elephant you will need one body, one head, two legs and two feet.
4 Ask a grown-up to help you cut some narrow slits in your shapes. Look at the pictures here to see where to make the slits.

5 Paint the pieces of your elephant grey and leave them to dry. If you don't have any grey paint, you could mix black and white together.
6 Slot the feet into the slits at the bottom of the leg shapes.

feet

leg

7 Slot all the other pieces together in the same way. Now, turn the page to see the finished elephant!

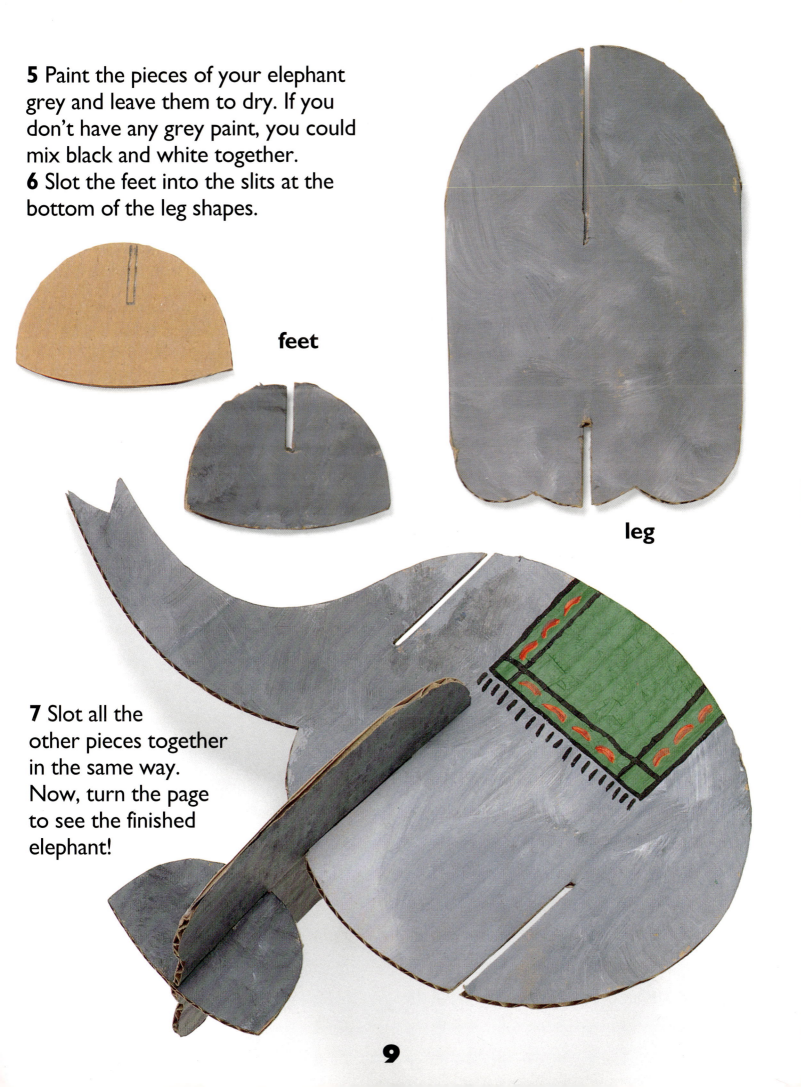

You can make all sorts of slit and slot models. We have made up another animal using slightly different shapes, slotted together in the same way. What sort of animal do you think it is?

Toy Town

This is a very easy way to make your own building blocks. You will be able to use them to create all sorts of different models.

Ready, steady, go...
1 Make a collection of old lids, cardboard tubes and boxes. The more shapes and sizes, the better!
2 Make sure that they are all clean.
3 Paint them in bright colours. You could paint zig-zags and dots on some, or you could paint them so that they look like real bricks.
4 Arrange your building blocks to make a model town.

You don't need to glue your blocks together, just balance them on top of each other. Can you think of any other kinds of models to make with your blocks?

Spotty Leopard

To make this jolly leopard, you will need a large cardboard box for the body and a smaller one for the head. Tear a few scraps of cardboard for the face, nose, ears, tongue and tail. It is easier to paint all the pieces before you stick them together.

3 Tear a rectangle of cardboard for the leopard's face, and another smaller piece for the nose.
4 Next, tear two more pieces of cardboard for the tongue and tail. Fold over the ends to make flaps.
5 Paint all of the pieces.

Ready, steady, go…
1 Start with the small box. Ask a grown-up to make a cut down the middle of each of the long sides. Look at the picture above and fold the box in half in the same way.
2 Tear two ears from cardboard. Bend the base of each ear over to make a flap.

6 Glue the two boxes together and then add all the other pieces. Use the flaps on the ears, tongue and tail to glue them to the head and body.

Salt Dough

Try making your own play dough. All you will need is 2 cups of plain flour, 1 cup of salt and roughly 1 cup of water. When you have made your dough you can shape it into some amazing creatures like the ones here.

Ready, steady, go…
1 Put the salt and flour into a bowl. Add the water slowly and use your hands to mix everything together. The dough should not be too sticky!

2 Take the dough out of the bowl and knead it on a table top for a few minutes. This will make it smooth and easy to model with.
3 Make a shape from your salt dough. You can add extra dough pieces, such as spikes. Push them gently on to your main model.

4 Put your finished model on a baking sheet. Ask a grown-up to bake it in an oven at the lowest temperature for about two hours.
5 When your model has cooled down you can paint it in bright colours. Turn the page and meet the rest of our monster family!

When you have made a few creatures, try setting them in a scene.
We made our 'rock pool' with some coloured paper and pebbles.

Nodding Bird

This colourful bird is easy to make. All you need is some thick cardboard, newspaper, flour and water paste, string and thick paint.

Ready, steady, go…
1 Use the bird shape here as a guide to trace around. Cut the shape out from the cardboard.
2 Cut out four cardboard rectangles for the legs and a long rectangle, like the one on the right, for the base.
3 Make some flour and water paste. Put half a mug of flour and a spoonful of salt in a bowl. Add some water and stir the mixture. Keep doing this until you have a thick, creamy paste.
4 Tear some strips of newspaper. Paste several layers round all of your shapes and leave them to dry.

body

leg

base

5 Ask a grown-up to poke two small holes in the base. The picture above shows where the holes should go.

7 Paint all of your cardboard shapes.
8 Use short lengths of string to put your bird and base together, like the one in the picture below.

6 You will also need two holes at the bottom of the bird's body and one at either end of each leg. The holes on the bird's body should be the same distance apart as the holes in the base.

9 Thread the lengths of string through the holes and make knots in the ends to stop them from slipping through. Hold your bird at the end of the base. Can you make it rock backwards and forwards?

Sticks and Stones

The next time you go for a walk in the garden or the park, keep your eyes open for interesting sticks and stones. Do not break branches off trees, and make sure you do not disturb any animals that might be hiding under stones!

Ready, steady, go...
1 Brush off any dirt or dust from your collection of sticks and stones.
2 Have a really good look at each one on its own.

3 When you have made up your mind what your stick looks like, you can paint it!
4 Use a chunky paintbrush and thick paint.

What animals do you think our stick models look like?
You could use your stick model to hang bangles, beads, or keys on.

We made our robin from a strange-looking stone. Can you think of any other way of painting the stone to make it look completely different?

Index

animals 5, 8, 9, 10, 11, 14, 15, 20, 21, 22, 23
building blocks 12, 13
cardboard 4, 5, 8, 12, 14, 20
monsters 6, 7, 16, 17, 18, 19
newspaper 20, 21
paint 4, 5, 9, 12, 14, 17, 20, 21, 22, 23
paste 20
pebbles 2, 3, 19, 22, 23
play dough 6, 7
salt dough 16, 17, 18, 19
split pins 4, 5
string 20, 21
wood 2, 22, 23

If you have enjoyed this book look out for the full range

PLAY & DISCOVER ◆ What We Eat ◆ Rain & Shine ◆ Growing Up ◆ What We Wear

CRAFT ◆ Paint ◆ Paper ◆ Dress Up ◆ Fun Food ◆ Models ◆ Papier-Mâché

ANIMALS ◆ Pets ◆ On Safari ◆ Underwater ◆ On the Farm ◆ Birds ◆ Animal Homes

First Published in Great Britain In 1994 by
Two-Can Publishing Ltd., 346 Old Street, London EC1V 9NQ
in association with Scholastic Publications Ltd.

Copyright © Two-Can Publishing Ltd. 1994

Printed and bound in Hong Kong   2 4 6 8 10 9 7 5 3 1

All rights reserved. No part of this publication may be reproduced, stored in a retrieval system, or transmitted in any form or by any means electronic, mechanical, photocopying, recording or otherwise, without the prior written permission of the copyright holder.

The JUMP! logo and the word JUMP! are registered trade marks.

A catalogue record for this book is available from the British Library

Pbk ISBN 1-85434-240-1
Hbk ISBN 1-85434-239-8

Photographs by Toby